Can You Say DINOSAUR?

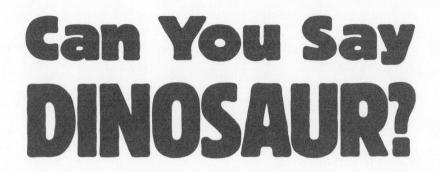

By Katharine Ross
Illustrations by Christopher Santoro

Learning Ladders/Random House

Manufactured in the United States of America   1 2 3 4 5 6 7 8 9 0

Can you say *dinosaur*? It's easier if you say it one bit at a time. DYE-no-sor. It means "terrible lizard." Long, long ago, before there were any people, dinosaurs roamed the earth.

The dinosaur in this picture is called *Stegosaurus*. Say it like this—stegg-uh-SOR-uss. See the row of funny-looking plates running down its back? Maybe the wind blowing through those plates kept it cool. Can you guess what the spikes on its tail were for? Maybe it used them to defend itself against other dinosaurs.

Some dinosaurs ate meat. Eating meat in those days meant eating insects, snakes, small lizards, fish, birds, or other dinosaurs. The little meat eater you see chasing a dragonfly is called *Saltopus*. Say SALT-o-pus. It means "leap-foot." And it had better leap quickly to get away from that big meat-eating *Allosaurus* (al-uh-SOR-uss).

Other dinosaurs ate plants. The dinosaurs grazing
here are called *Camptosaurus*. Say it like this—
KAMP-tuh-sor-uss. It means "bent lizard." They got
this name because they had to bend down on all fours
to eat grass.

Who was the largest dinosaur of all time? Say bron-tuh-SOR-uss. *Brontosaurus* means "thunder lizard." Those four huge feet hitting the ground must have made a noise like thunder. Its long neck helped it reach leaves on high trees. A full-grown *Brontosaurus* probably had to eat 700 pounds of leaves a day. Imagine if you had to eat 1,000 boxes of cereal every day just to keep going.

The biggest, strongest, fiercest meat eater ever to live was *Tyrannosaurus rex*. When you say tie-ran-uh-SOR-uss REX, you are saying "king of the tyrant lizards." It was bigger than a house and had teeth as long and sharp as carving knives. Other dinosaurs must have run for their lives when they saw it coming.

One little dinosaur was too slow to outrun
Tyrannosaurus, but it had ways of protecting itself.
Its name is *Ankylosaurus*.
Can you say an-kie-luh-SOR-uss?
It was built like an army tank
and was probably too tough to
chew.

Some dinosaurs had bills and webbed feet, like ducks. *Parasaurolophus* is the name of one of these dinosaurs. Say par-ah-sor-OL-uh-fus. Quite a mouthful, isn't it?

That's *Triceratops* (try-SER-uh-tops) with the three horns. It buried its eggs in the sand to keep them safe. Can you guess from whom it was hiding them? It was that *Oviraptor* hiding in the bushes. Can you say o-vee-RAP-tor? That's a good name for it, all right. It means "egg thief."

How do we know that dinosaurs once lived? We know about dinosaurs from bones that scientists have found buried deep in the ground. When scientists fit these bones together, they make a skeleton. The skeleton tells them what the dinosaur looked like when it was alive.

Why are there no dinosaurs alive today? Scientists can only guess. But it's fun to say their long, tongue-twisting names. And it's fascinating to look at their bones and imagine what life was like when dinosaurs roamed the earth.